DR SAMUEL JAMES

ARTIFICIAL INTELLIGENCE IN MEDICINE

A COMPREHENSIVE GUIDE FOR AI CLINICAL INNOVATION AND PRECISION MEDICINE

2025

Artificial Intelligence in Medicine: A Comprehensive Guide for AI Clinical Innovation and Precision Medicine

Dr. Samuel James

———

Global M.B.A, (Deakin University, Australia),

PGP Management (IMT Ghaziabad),

PGD Hospital Management (Madurai Kamarajar University, India)

Change Management (Johns Hopkins Universitym USA)

M.B.B.S (JIPMER, Pondicherry, India)

Clinical Ordinatura Diagnostic Radiology (Dnipro Medical Academy, Ukraine)

Contents

Book Introduction

———

Artificial Intelligence (AI) is fundamentally transforming the landscape of healthcare, offering innovative solutions that enhance patient care, streamline clinical processes, and facilitate precision medicine. This comprehensive guide aims to explore the multifaceted applications of AI in medicine, providing healthcare professionals, researchers, and policymakers with essential insights into this rapidly evolving field.

Part I: Introduction to AI Disruption in Healthcare

The first part of this book serves as an introduction to the role of AI in healthcare. It begins with a foundational overview of AI technologies and their significance in revolutionizing clinical practices. The chapters delve into the core technologies driving AI advancements, including machine learning, natural language processing, and robotics. Understanding these technologies is crucial for grasping how they can be harnessed to improve healthcare delivery.

Part II: AI in Clinical Practice

In this section, the focus shifts to the practical applications of AI within clinical settings. It covers **AI-Enhanced Diagnostics**, which explores how AI algorithms can assist in interpreting medical images and diagnosing conditions with greater accuracy. The section also discusses **AI in Clinical Decision Support**, highlighting how AI tools can provide evidence-based recommendations to clinicians, ultimately improving patient outcomes. Furthermore, it addresses the integration of AI into **Precision Medicine**, showcasing how personalized treatment plans can be developed by analyzing individual patient data.

Part III: AI in Patient Care and Monitoring

This part examines the impact of AI on patient care and monitoring systems. It discusses **AI-Powered Remote Care**, which allows for continuous monitoring of patients outside traditional healthcare settings, thereby enhancing accessibility and convenience. The chapter on **Predictive Analytics** illustrates how AI can forecast health events and trends, enabling proactive interventions. Additionally, it explores the potential of AI to streamline administrative processes and optimize resource management within healthcare organizations.

Part IV: The Future of AI in Healthcare

The final section looks ahead to emerging trends and technologies that will shape the future of healthcare. It discusses the challenges associated with implementing AI solutions, including ethical considerations and integration hurdles. The book concludes with strategies for preparing healthcare systems for an AI-enabled future, emphasizing the importance of interdisciplinary collaboration and continuous innovation.This guide is essential for anyone involved in healthcare as it not only highlights the transformative potential of AI but also provides practical insights into its implementation and future directions. By understanding these dynamics, stakeholders can better navigate the complexities of integrating AI into clinical practice, ultimately improving patient care and outcomes in a rapidly changing medical landscape.

Part I: Introduction to AI Disruption in Healthcare

Chapter 1: Introduction to AI in Healthcare

―――――

The evolution of artificial intelligence (AI) in medicine has been a remarkable journey, transforming healthcare practices and opening new frontiers in patient care. From its nascent stages in the mid-20th century to its current sophisticated applications, AI has steadily integrated into various aspects of healthcare, promising to revolutionize how we approach diagnosis, treatment, and overall patient management.

The roots of AI in medicine can be traced back to the 1960s when researchers began exploring the potential of computer-assisted diagnosis. Early systems like MYCIN, developed for diagnosing blood infections, laid the groundwork for future AI applications in healthcare (Shortliffe, 1976). As computational power increased and algorithms became more sophisticated, the 1980s and 1990s saw the emergence of expert systems and neural networks in medical decision-making processes.

The turn of the millennium marked a significant acceleration in AI's medical applications. With the advent of big data and machine learning, AI systems began demonstrating remarkable capabilities in analyzing complex medical data. For instance, AI algorithms have shown prowess in interpreting medical images, often matching or surpassing human experts in accuracy (Topol, 2019).

Current applications of AI in healthcare span a wide spectrum, from administrative tasks to clinical decision support. In diagnostics, AI-powered tools are enhancing the accuracy of image interpretation in radiology and pathology. For example, AI algorithms can now detect early signs of breast cancer in mammograms with high precision, potentially leading to earlier interventions and improved patient outcomes (McKinney et al., 2020).

In the realm of personalized medicine, AI is facilitating the analysis of vast genomic datasets, enabling tailored treatment plans based on an individual's genetic profile. This approach holds immense promise for oncology, where AI can help identify the most effective therapies for specific cancer types (Xu et al., 2019).

Administrative efficiency has also seen significant improvements through AI implementation. Natural language processing (NLP) technologies are streamlining electronic health record (EHR) management, reducing the administrative burden on healthcare professionals and allowing more time for patient care (Rajkomar et al., 2018).

Looking to the future, AI's potential in healthcare appears boundless. Predictive analytics powered by AI could revolutionize preventive care, identifying at-risk patients before symptoms manifest. In drug discovery, AI algorithms are accelerating the process of identifying potential drug candidates, potentially reducing the time and cost of bringing new treatments to market (Vamathevan et al., 2019).

However, it's crucial to note that while AI holds immense promise, its integration into healthcare must be approached with caution and ethical consideration. Issues of data privacy, algorithmic bias, and the need for human oversight remain paramount concerns that need to be addressed as AI continues to evolve in the medical field.

AI's role in achieving healthcare's quadruple aim - enhancing patient experience, improving population health, reducing costs, and improving the work life of healthcare providers - is becoming increasingly evident. By automating routine tasks, providing decision support, and enabling more precise and personalized care, AI is contributing to each of these goals. For instance, AI-powered chatbots are improving patient engagement and access to health information, while predictive models are helping to manage population health more effectively (Meskó et al., 2018).

In conclusion, the journey of AI in healthcare has been one of continuous evolution and expanding potential. As we stand on the cusp of a new era in medicine, the integration of AI promises to enhance our ability to provide high-quality, efficient, and personalized healthcare. However, this integration must be guided by ethical considerations and a commitment to maintaining the human touch that is so crucial in medicine.

References:

McKinney, S.M. et al. (2020) 'International evaluation of an AI system for breast cancer screening', Nature, 577(7788), pp. 89-94.

Meskó, B. et al. (2018) 'Digital health is a cultural transformation of traditional healthcare', mHealth, 4, p. 38.

Rajkomar, A. et al. (2018) 'Scalable and accurate deep learning with electronic health records', npj Digital Medicine, 1(1), p. 18.

Shortliffe, E.H. (1976) Computer-based medical consultations: MYCIN. New York: Elsevier.

Topol, E.J. (2019) 'High-performance medicine: the convergence of human and artificial intelligence', Nature Medicine, 25(1), pp. 44-56.

Vamathevan, J. et al. (2019) 'Applications of machine learning in drug discovery and development', Nature Reviews Drug Discovery, 18(6), pp. 463-477.

Xu, J. et al. (2019) 'Translating cancer genomics into precision medicine with artificial intelligence: applications, challenges and future perspectives', Human Genetics, 138(2), pp. 109-124.

Chapter 2: Core AI Technologies in Healthcare

Artificial Intelligence (AI) in healthcare encompasses several key technologies that are revolutionizing medical practice. This chapter explores three core AI technologies: machine learning and deep learning, natural language processing, and computer vision and image analysis. These technologies are transforming how healthcare professionals diagnose, treat, and manage patient care.

Machine Learning and Deep Learning

Machine learning (ML) is a subset of AI that enables computers to learn from data without being explicitly programmed. In healthcare, ML algorithms can analyze vast amounts of medical data to identify patterns and make predictions. For instance, ML can predict patient outcomes, recommend personalized treatment plans, or identify high-risk patients for early intervention (Topol, 2019).

Deep learning, a more advanced form of machine learning, uses artificial neural networks inspired by the human brain's structure. These networks can process complex, unstructured data such as medical images or patient records with remarkable accuracy. For example, deep learning algorithms have shown the ability to detect breast cancer in mammograms with greater accuracy than human radiologists (McKinney et al., 2020).

One practical application of deep learning in healthcare is in diabetes management. Medtronic's Guardian Connect system uses deep learning to predict blood glucose levels in diabetic patients, alerting them about potential hypoglycemic events up to an hour in advance (Appinventiv, 2024). This proactive approach allows for timely intervention and better disease management.

Natural Language Processing

Natural Language Processing (NLP) is an AI technology that enables computers to understand, interpret, and generate human language. In healthcare, NLP is particularly valuable for processing and analyzing unstructured text data, such as clinical notes, medical literature, and patient records.

NLP can automate clinical documentation, extract relevant information from electronic health records (EHRs), and assist in medical coding. For instance, NLP algorithms can analyze clinical notes to identify key symptoms, diagnoses, and treatments, saving healthcare providers significant time and reducing administrative burden (ForeSee Medical, 2025).

Moreover, NLP powers advanced clinical decision support systems. These systems can analyze vast amounts of medical literature and patient data to provide evidence-based recommendations to healthcare providers. For example, IBM Watson uses NLP to analyze medical literature and patient data to suggest personalized cancer treatment options (Research.aimultiple.com, 2024).

Computer Vision and Image Analysis

Computer vision is an AI technology that enables machines to interpret and analyze visual information from the world. In healthcare, computer vision is primarily applied to medical imaging, revolutionizing how healthcare professionals interpret and utilize medical images.

Computer vision algorithms can analyze various medical images, including X-rays, CT scans, MRIs, and ultrasounds, to detect abnormalities and assist in diagnosis. For instance, AI-powered systems have demonstrated remarkable accuracy in detecting lung diseases from chest X-rays and identifying early signs of diabetic retinopathy in retinal images (PixelPlex, 2024).

A notable example of computer vision in healthcare is Viz.ai's stroke care platform. This system uses AI to analyze CT scans of the brain, quickly identifying potential stroke cases and alerting specialists. This application has been shown to reduce the time to treatment for stroke patients by 1.5 hours, potentially improving outcomes significantly (Topflightapps, 2024).

These core AI technologies are not isolated; they often work in synergy to provide comprehensive healthcare solutions. For instance, a system might use computer vision to analyze medical images, deep learning to interpret the results, and NLP to generate a human-readable report for healthcare providers.

As these technologies continue to evolve, they promise to enhance diagnostic accuracy, improve treatment efficacy, and ultimately lead to better patient outcomes. However, it's crucial to note that while AI technologies offer powerful tools, they are designed to augment, not replace, the expertise of healthcare professionals. The human touch in healthcare remains irreplaceable, with AI serving as a valuable aid in decision-making and patient care.

References:

Appinventiv (2024) 'NLP in Healthcare: Transforming Patient Care & Efficiency', 2 September. Available at: https://appinventiv.com/blog/nlp-in-healthcare/ (Accessed: 23 January 2025).

ForeSee Medical (2025) 'Natural Language Processing in Healthcare', ForeSee Medical. Available at: https://www.foreseemed.com/natural-language-processing-in-healthcare (Accessed: 23 January 2025).

McKinney, S.M. et al. (2020) 'International evaluation of an AI system for breast cancer screening', Nature, 577(7788), pp. 89-94.

PixelPlex (2024) 'Computer Vision in Healthcare: 8 Promising Applications', 8 October. Available at: https://pixelplex.io/blog/computer-vision-in-healthcare/ (Accessed: 23 January 2025).

Research.aimultiple.com (2024) '12 Real-Life Applications of Deep Learning in Healthcare ['25]', 11 December. Available at: https://research.aimultiple.com/deep-learning-in-healthcare/ (Accessed: 23 January 2025).

Topflightapps (2024) 'Computer Vision in the Medical Field Transforms Healthcare', 18 November. Available at: https://topflightapps.com/ideas/computer-vision-in-medicine/ (Accessed: 23 January 2025).

Topol, E.J. (2019) 'High-performance medicine: the convergence of human and artificial intelligence', Nature Medicine, 25(1), pp. 44-56.

Part II: AI in Clinical Practice

Chapter 3: AI-Enhanced Diagnostics

Artificial Intelligence (AI) is revolutionizing clinical practice, particularly in the realm of diagnostics. This chapter explores the applications of AI in medical imaging, early disease detection, risk prediction, and the associated challenges and limitations.

AI in Medical Imaging

AI has made significant strides in medical imaging, encompassing radiology, pathology, and dermatology. In radiology, AI algorithms can analyze large volumes of imaging data, identifying patterns and abnormalities that might be overlooked by human eyes (Spectral AI, 2024). For instance, AI-powered systems have demonstrated remarkable accuracy in detecting lung diseases from chest X-rays and identifying early signs of diabetic retinopathy in retinal images (PixelPlex, 2024).

In pathology, AI assists in identifying cancerous cells in biopsy samples, improving early detection and treatment planning. These AI tools can expedite image analysis, allowing pathologists to focus on complex cases and reduce diagnostic errors (Spectral AI, 2024).

Dermatology has also benefited from AI advancements. Google Health has developed AI tools to improve access to skin disease information, potentially aiding in early diagnosis of skin conditions (Google Health, 2025).

AI for Early Disease Detection and Risk Prediction

One of the most promising applications of AI in healthcare is its ability to predict diseases and identify risk factors years before symptoms appear. For example, researchers at UC San Francisco have developed a machine learning model that can predict

Alzheimer's disease up to seven years before symptoms manifest by analyzing patient records (UCSF, 2024).

Similarly, scientists using AI to analyze blood samples have been able to predict a person's risk of developing conditions such as Alzheimer's and heart disease up to a decade in advance. This approach involves identifying patterns of proteins in the blood linked to increased disease risk (University of Edinburgh, 2024).

In cardiovascular health, AI algorithms can identify individuals at risk of cardiovascular disease (CVD), allowing for early intervention to change the disease trajectory (Nature, 2024). This capability is particularly crucial given the global burden of CVD and the potential for prevention through early risk assessment.

Challenges and Limitations of AI Diagnostics

Despite its potential, AI in diagnostics faces several challenges and limitations. One significant concern is the issue of bias in AI algorithms. AI models trained on non-diverse datasets may perform poorly when applied to underrepresented populations, potentially exacerbating healthcare disparities (Nature, 2024).

Another challenge is the integration of AI tools into existing clinical workflows. While AI can enhance efficiency, it requires careful implementation to ensure it complements rather than disrupts established practices. Healthcare providers need proper training to effectively use and interpret AI-generated insights (Deloitte, 2025).

Data privacy and security also present significant challenges. As AI systems rely on large datasets, ensuring the confidentiality and integrity of patient information is paramount. Robust data governance frameworks are necessary to maintain patient trust and comply with regulatory requirements.

Lastly, while AI shows promise in many diagnostic areas, it is not infallible. The "black box" nature of some AI algorithms can make it difficult for healthcare providers to understand and explain the reasoning behind AI-generated diagnoses. This lack of explainability can be problematic in clinical settings where transparency is crucial (Forbes, 2024).

In conclusion, AI-enhanced diagnostics offer tremendous potential to improve patient care through early detection, accurate diagnosis, and personalized risk prediction. However, addressing the challenges of bias, integration, data security, and explainability is crucial for the responsible and effective implementation of AI in clinical practice. As these technologies continue to evolve, ongoing research, ethical considerations, and collaborative efforts between AI developers and healthcare professionals will be essential to harness the full potential of AI in diagnostics while ensuring patient safety and care quality.

References:

Deloitte (2025) Accelerating medical imaging diagnostics using AI. Available at: https://www2.deloitte.com/us/en/pages/consulting/articles/google-cloud-alliance-medical-diagnostics-using-ai.html (Accessed: 23 January 2025).

Forbes (2024) 'Transforming Radiology With AI-Powered Diagnostics', 29 September. Available at: https://www.forbes.com/sites/tonybradley/2024/09/29/transforming-radiology-with-ai-powered-diagnostics/ (Accessed: 23 January 2025).

Google Health (2025) AI Imaging & Diagnostics. Available at: https://health.google/health-research/imaging-and-diagnostics/ (Accessed: 23 January 2025).

Nature (2024) 'Artificial intelligence bias in the prediction and detection of cardiovascular disease', 21 November. Available at: https://www.nature.com/articles/s44325-024-00031-9 (Accessed: 23 January 2025).

PixelPlex (2024) 'Computer Vision in Healthcare: 8 Promising Applications', 8 October. Available at: https://pixelplex.io/blog/computer-vision-in-healthcare/ (Accessed: 23 January 2025).

Spectral AI (2024) 'Artificial Intelligence in Medical Imaging', 16 August. Available at: https://www.spectral-ai.com/blog/artificial-intelligence-in-medical-imaging/ (Accessed: 23 January 2025).

UCSF (2024) 'How AI Can Help Spot Early Risk Factors for Alzheimer's Disease', 21 February. Available at: https://www.ucsf.edu/news/2024/02/427131/how-ai-can-help-spot-early-risk-factors-alzheimers-disease (Accessed: 23 January 2025).

University of Edinburgh (2024) 'AI insights predict disease a decade in advance', 30 July. Available at: https://www.ed.ac.uk/news/2024/ai-insights-predict-disease-a-decade-in-advance (Accessed: 23 January 2025).

Chapter 4: AI in Clinical Decision Support

Artificial Intelligence (AI) is revolutionizing clinical decision support, offering powerful tools to assist healthcare professionals in making more informed and accurate decisions. This chapter explores AI-powered clinical decision tools, their impact on diagnostic accuracy, and the potential risks associated with biased AI models.

AI-powered Clinical Decision Tools

Clinical Decision Support Systems (CDSS) have long been a part of healthcare, but the integration of AI has significantly enhanced their capabilities. AI-powered CDSS can analyze vast amounts of patient data, including medical records, recent studies, and clinical guidelines, to provide real-time advice and treatment options tailored to each patient (ACM, 2024). These systems utilize advanced algorithms, particularly large language models (LLMs), which can understand and process natural language used in medical records and clinical studies.

For example, when a doctor inputs a patient's symptoms, the AI-powered CDSS can rapidly sift through extensive medical data to generate a list of possible diagnoses, recommended tests, or treatment plans. This process is akin to having a highly knowledgeable colleague available to confirm or challenge the doctor's initial assessment, ultimately leading to more confident decision-making and reduced time spent on administrative tasks (ACM, 2024).

Improving Diagnostic Accuracy with AI

AI has demonstrated remarkable potential in enhancing diagnostic accuracy across various medical fields. In radiology, AI algorithms have shown the ability to analyze medical images with a level of precision that often surpasses human experts (Park, 2024). This capability has led to earlier detection of diseases, improving patient outcomes and survival rates.

A notable example is in cardiology, where AI has been used to interpret electrocardiograms (ECGs). In a study by Hannun et al. (2019), deep neural network models outperformed cardiologists in diagnosing ECG abnormalities and arrhythmias. The AI models achieved an average area under the receiver operating characteristic curve of 0.97 and an average F1 score of 0.837, surpassing the average cardiologist score of 0.780 (NCBI, 2024). These results suggest that AI has the potential to enhance the efficiency and accuracy of ECG analysis, potentially reducing incorrect diagnoses and supporting expert-human ECG interpretation by prioritizing urgent cases.

AI's impact on diagnostic accuracy extends beyond cardiology. In oncology, AI is enabling personalized cancer treatments through genomic analysis, identifying mutations, and tailoring therapies to a patient's unique cancer profile. This approach not only improves treatment efficacy but also reduces side effects and accelerates drug discovery (World Economic Forum, 2025).

Potential Risks of Biased AI Models

While AI offers significant benefits in clinical decision support, it is crucial to address the potential risks associated with biased AI models. Bias in AI algorithms can perpetuate or even exacerbate existing health disparities, particularly affecting disadvantaged populations (HHS, 2023).

One primary source of bias is the lack of diversity in the data used to train AI models. When AI systems are developed using data predominantly from certain demographic groups, they may perform poorly when applied to underrepresented populations. For instance, an AI algorithm trained primarily on data from white patients might not perform as accurately when diagnosing or recommending treatments for patients from other racial or ethnic backgrounds (Nature, 2023).

Another concern is the potential for AI models to reflect and amplify existing societal biases. For example, if an AI system is trained on historical healthcare data that reflects systemic inequalities in healthcare access and expenditures, it may inadvertently perpetuate these disparities in its recommendations (Nature, 2023).

The implications of biased AI models in healthcare can be severe. They may lead to misdiagnoses, delayed treatments, or inappropriate care recommendations for certain patient groups. For instance, a study at Rutgers University-Newark found that AI algorithms used in healthcare could have biases and blind spots that impede healthcare for Black and Latinx patients, potentially leading to misdiagnosis or delays in treatment (Rutgers University-Newark, 2024).

To mitigate these risks, it is crucial to implement strategies such as using diverse training data, incorporating bias detection and mitigation techniques in AI development, and maintaining human oversight in clinical decision-making. Additionally, increasing diversity among AI developers and healthcare professionals can help ensure that AI systems are designed with a broader range of perspectives and experiences in mind (Rutgers University-Newark, 2024).

In conclusion, while AI-powered clinical decision support tools offer immense potential for improving diagnostic accuracy and patient care, it is essential to approach their development and implementation with caution. By addressing the challenges of bias and ensuring ethical, inclusive AI development, we can harness the full potential of AI to enhance clinical decision-making and improve healthcare outcomes for all patients.

Chapter 5: Precision Medicine and AI

P recision medicine, a healthcare approach that tailors medical treatments to individual patients based on their unique genetic, environmental, and lifestyle factors, has been revolutionized by the integration of Artificial Intelligence (AI). This chapter explores how AI is transforming personalized treatment planning, genomics and proteomics analysis, and drug discovery and development.

Personalized Treatment Planning

AI has significantly enhanced the ability to create personalized treatment plans for patients. By analyzing vast amounts of patient data, including genetic information, clinical history, and lifestyle factors, AI algorithms can generate tailored treatment recommendations that are more effective and have fewer side effects than traditional one-size-fits-all approaches (Gaper.io, 2024).

For instance, AI-powered systems can analyze a patient's genetic profile, medical history, and current health status to predict how they might respond to different treatments. This capability allows healthcare providers to select the most appropriate therapy for each individual, potentially improving outcomes and reducing adverse effects. In oncology, for example, AI is enabling personalized cancer treatments through genomic analysis, identifying specific mutations, and tailoring therapies to a patient's unique cancer profile (World Economic Forum, 2025).

Moreover, AI facilitates real-time monitoring of patients through wearable devices and sensors. These devices collect data on vital signs, activity levels, and other relevant metrics, which AI algorithms can analyze to provide continuous feedback on a patient's health status. This real-time monitoring empowers healthcare professionals to make timely interventions and adjustments to treatment plans as needed (Gaper.io, 2024).

AI in Genomics and Proteomics

The fields of genomics and proteomics have been transformed by AI, enabling more comprehensive and nuanced understanding of human biology at the molecular level. In genomics, AI algorithms can analyze vast amounts of genetic data to identify disease risks, potential treatment options, and enable precision medicine approaches (Gaper.io, 2024).

Proteomics, the study of proteins in biological systems, has also benefited significantly from AI integration. Unlike the genome, which remains relatively static throughout an individual's lifetime, the proteome - all the proteins in a cell or tissue - is in constant flux, adapting to changing conditions. AI algorithms can analyze this complex, dynamic system to provide insights into an individual's health status at any given time (Medical Xpress, 2024).

A notable example of AI's application in proteomics is the π-HuB (The Proteomic Navigator of the Human Body) project. This ambitious initiative aims to create a 3D digital representation of human organs, tissues, body fluids, and cells over time, enabling prediction of complex diseases and impacts of non-genetic factors on health. By integrating AI with proteomic data, researchers hope to improve disease diagnosis, treatment, and prevention strategies (Medical Xpress, 2024).

Drug Discovery and Development Using AI

AI is revolutionizing the drug discovery and development process, potentially reducing the time and cost of bringing new treatments to market. Traditional drug discovery methods often involve a time-consuming and expensive process of trial and error. AI can significantly streamline this process by analyzing vast amounts of biological and chemical data to identify promising drug candidates more quickly and accurately.

One example of AI's impact on drug discovery is the PIONEER (Protein-protein InteractiOn iNtErfacE pRediction) tool developed by scientists at Cleveland Clinic and Cornell University. This AI-powered system can predict how DNA mutations influence protein-

protein interactions, which is crucial for identifying potential drug targets. PIONEER's database allows researchers to navigate the interactome - the whole set of molecular interactions in a cell - for more than 10,500 diseases, significantly accelerating the drug discovery process (Cleveland Clinic, 2024).

AI algorithms can also analyze data from previous clinical trials, scientific literature, and molecular databases to predict how new compounds might behave in the human body. This predictive capability can help researchers prioritize which compounds to test in clinical trials, potentially saving time and resources in the drug development process.

Furthermore, AI can assist in designing more effective clinical trials by identifying optimal patient populations, predicting potential side effects, and suggesting the most appropriate dosing regimens. This application of AI not only accelerates the drug development process but also increases the likelihood of successful trials and ultimately, the approval of new treatments (NCBI, 2020).

In conclusion, the integration of AI into precision medicine is ushering in a new era of personalized healthcare. By enabling more accurate and tailored treatment plans, advancing our understanding of genomics and proteomics, and accelerating drug discovery and development, AI is transforming the landscape of medical care. As these technologies continue to evolve, they promise to deliver more effective, efficient, and personalized healthcare solutions, ultimately improving patient outcomes and quality of life.

References:

Cleveland Clinic (2024) 'New AI tool predicts protein-protein interaction mutations in hundreds of diseases', 24 October. Available at:
https://www.lerner.ccf.org/news/article/?title=New+AI+tool+predict s+protein-
protein+interaction+mutations+in+hundreds+of+diseases&id=8f8ae 79a0e14e0f074307238dd2423b74f3ee925 (Accessed: 23 January 2025).

Gaper.io (2024) 'The Role of AI in Personalized Healthcare', 3 February. Available at: https://gaper.io/role-of-ai-in-personalized-healthcare/ (Accessed: 23 January 2025).

Medical Xpress (2024) 'Proteomics and AI unite for a new era in medicine and health care', 12 December. Available at: https://medicalxpress.com/news/2024-12-proteomics-ai-era-medicine-health.html (Accessed: 23 January 2025).

NCBI (2020) 'Precision Medicine, AI, and the Future of Personalized Health Care', 12 October. Available at: https://pmc.ncbi.nlm.nih.gov/articles/PMC7877825/ (Accessed: 23 January 2025).

World Economic Forum (2025) 'AI in Personalized Healthcare'. [No URL available] (Accessed: 23 January 2025).

Part III: AI in Patient Care and Monitoring

Chapter 6: AI-Powered Remote Care

The integration of Artificial Intelligence (AI) in remote healthcare has revolutionized patient care and monitoring, offering innovative solutions that bridge the gap between healthcare providers and patients. This chapter explores three key areas where AI is transforming remote care: telemedicine and virtual health assistants, wearable devices for continuous monitoring, and AI chatbots for patient engagement.

Telemedicine and Virtual Health Assistants

Telemedicine, the practice of providing healthcare remotely using telecommunications technology, has been significantly enhanced by AI. AI-powered telemedicine platforms are now capable of facilitating more efficient and effective remote consultations between healthcare providers and patients. These systems utilize predictive analytics and machine learning algorithms to improve the accuracy of remote diagnoses and treatment recommendations1.

Virtual health assistants, often in the form of AI-powered chatbots, play a crucial role in telemedicine by managing administrative tasks and enhancing patient interactions. These assistants can handle appointment scheduling, insurance verification, and documentation, allowing healthcare providers to focus more on patient care2. For instance, virtual medical assistants can prepare patients for telemedicine consultations by providing pre-consultation instructions and explaining treatment protocols, thereby improving patient understanding and compliance with treatment plans6.

Moreover, AI-enabled virtual triage systems analyze patient symptoms and data to prioritize cases based on urgency, ensuring timely care for critical conditions and optimizing healthcare provider workflows5. This AI-driven approach not only improves the efficiency of telemedicine services but also enhances patient satisfaction by reducing wait times and providing immediate, relevant information.

Wearable Devices and Continuous Monitoring

Wearable health devices, empowered by AI, have become instrumental in chronic disease management and preventive healthcare. These devices offer real-time, continuous monitoring of various health parameters, providing valuable data that enables early detection of potential health issues and facilitates timely interventions[7].

For example, in cardiology, wearable devices equipped with AI algorithms can monitor heart rate, blood pressure, and even perform ECG analysis. This continuous monitoring allows for the early detection of arrhythmias and other cardiac abnormalities, potentially preventing serious cardiovascular events[7]. Similarly, in diabetes management, AI-powered continuous glucose monitors provide real-time glucose readings, enabling more precise insulin dosing and improved glycemic control.

The integration of AI with wearable technology extends beyond individual device capabilities. AI algorithms can analyze data from multiple wearable devices to provide a comprehensive view of a patient's health status. This holistic approach to health monitoring enables healthcare providers to develop more personalized and effective treatment plans[3].

AI Chatbots for Patient Engagement

AI chatbots have emerged as powerful tools for enhancing patient engagement and improving healthcare outcomes. These intelligent systems can provide 24/7 support to patients, answering questions, offering health information, and even assisting with symptom checking and triage[8].

One of the most impactful applications of AI chatbots in healthcare is in appointment management. These systems can automatically book appointments, confirm availability, and send reminders to patients, significantly reducing no-show rates and improving overall healthcare efficiency[8]. For instance, chatbots like Ada Health have demonstrated the ability to integrate these functionalities seamlessly, helping patients manage their healthcare more effectively while reducing the administrative burden on healthcare staff.

AI chatbots also play a crucial role in patient education and health promotion. They can provide personalized health information, explain treatment plans, and encourage patients to adopt healthier lifestyles6. This continuous engagement and education can lead to improved treatment adherence and better health outcomes.

Furthermore, AI chatbots have shown particular promise in engaging older adults with healthcare technology. A study found that individuals over 60 using chatbots for health information reported a low cognitive load, indicating that these systems can be user-friendly and accessible to diverse patient populations8.

In conclusion, AI-powered remote care technologies are transforming the healthcare landscape, offering new possibilities for continuous, personalized, and efficient patient care. As these technologies continue to evolve, they promise to further enhance the quality and accessibility of healthcare, ultimately leading to improved patient outcomes and experiences.

Chapter 7: Predictive Analytics in Healthcare

P redictive analytics in healthcare has emerged as a powerful tool for improving patient outcomes, optimizing resource allocation, and shifting towards proactive care models. This chapter explores three key applications of predictive analytics in healthcare: early warning systems for clinical deterioration, population health management, and proactive and preventative care strategies.

Early Warning Systems for Clinical Deterioration

Early Warning Systems (EWS) are tools designed to identify patients at risk of clinical deterioration, enabling timely intervention and potentially preventing adverse outcomes. These systems typically use a combination of physiological parameters, such as blood pressure, heart rate, respiratory rate, and level of consciousness, to calculate a composite score that indicates a patient's risk level6.

The concept of EWS originated in 1997 and has since evolved to include various iterations tailored for different clinical settings and patient populations2. The primary goal of these systems is to standardize the process of identifying at-risk patients and facilitate rapid, appropriate escalation of care.

One of the key strengths of EWS is their ability to detect subtle changes in a patient's condition up to 24 hours before a serious clinical event occurs10. This early detection window allows healthcare providers to intervene proactively, potentially reducing the need for intensive care unit admissions, decreasing hospital length of stay, and even preventing cardiac arrests or deaths.

In practice, EWS are often integrated into electronic health record systems, allowing for continuous monitoring and automatic alerts when a patient's score exceeds a predetermined threshold. This integration enables healthcare providers to respond quickly to deteriorating patients, improving the overall quality of care and patient safety.

Population Health Management

Population health management is an approach that aims to improve the health outcomes of entire groups of individuals, often defined by geographic areas, specific health conditions, or demographic characteristics. Predictive analytics plays a crucial role in this field by enabling healthcare organizations to identify high-risk individuals within populations and implement targeted interventions7.

By analyzing large datasets that include clinical, demographic, and socioeconomic information, predictive analytics can help healthcare providers anticipate future health trends and allocate resources more effectively. For example, these tools can identify patients at high risk of developing chronic conditions, allowing for early intervention and potentially preventing the onset of disease3.

One of the key benefits of using predictive analytics in population health management is improved resource allocation. By understanding the health needs and risks of specific populations, healthcare organizations can focus their efforts and resources where they are likely to have the greatest impact7. This targeted approach not only improves patient outcomes but also helps to optimize healthcare spending and reduce overall costs.

Proactive and Preventative Care Strategies

The shift from reactive to proactive healthcare models represents a significant paradigm change in the medical field. Proactive care focuses on preventing diseases and maintaining health rather than simply treating illnesses as they occur. Predictive analytics plays a vital role in enabling this transition by providing insights that allow healthcare providers to anticipate and address potential health issues before they become severe4.

One example of proactive care enabled by predictive analytics is the use of risk assessment models to identify patients who may be at high risk for certain conditions. For instance, healthcare providers can use predictive models to identify patients who are likely to need hip replacement surgery in the future, allowing for early intervention and potentially delaying or preventing the need for surgery4.

Preventative care strategies, such as regular check-ups, screenings, and vaccinations, are also enhanced by predictive analytics. By analyzing patient data, healthcare providers can determine which preventative measures are most appropriate for individual patients based on their unique risk factors and health history8.

Furthermore, predictive analytics can help healthcare organizations implement more effective patient engagement strategies. By identifying patients who are at risk of non-compliance with treatment plans or who may be likely to miss appointments, providers can implement targeted interventions to improve patient adherence and overall health outcomes4.

In conclusion, predictive analytics is transforming healthcare by enabling early identification of clinical deterioration, improving population health management, and facilitating proactive and preventative care strategies. As these technologies continue to evolve and integrate with existing healthcare systems, they promise to enhance patient care, improve outcomes, and optimize resource utilization across the healthcare spectrum.

Chapter 8: Streamlining Administrative Processes

———

The integration of Artificial Intelligence (AI) in healthcare administration has revolutionized the way medical institutions manage their operations. This chapter explores three key areas where AI is transforming administrative processes: automated documentation and transcription, appointment scheduling and patient communication, and clinical coding and billing optimization.

Automated Documentation and Transcription

One of the most time-consuming tasks for healthcare providers is documentation. AI-powered systems are now capable of automating much of this process, significantly reducing the administrative burden on medical staff. These systems use natural language processing (NLP) and machine learning algorithms to convert spoken words into written text, creating accurate and detailed medical records in real-time.

For instance, AI-based transcription tools can listen to doctor-patient conversations and automatically generate clinical notes. This not only saves time but also improves the accuracy and completeness of medical records. Healthcare providers can focus more on patient care rather than spending hours on paperwork, leading to increased efficiency and potentially better patient outcomes1.

Moreover, these AI systems can learn from patterns in medical records to suggest relevant information for inclusion, ensuring that important details are not overlooked. This capability is particularly valuable in maintaining comprehensive and consistent patient records across different healthcare providers and specialties.

AI in Appointment Scheduling and Patient Communication

AI has transformed the way healthcare facilities manage appointments and communicate with patients. AI-powered scheduling systems can analyze vast amounts of data, including patient preferences, provider availability, and resource allocation, to optimize appointment scheduling2.

These systems can automatically assign appointments based on urgency, patient history, and provider specialization. For example, a patient with a history of cardiac issues might be prioritized for an earlier appointment with a cardiologist. This intelligent scheduling not only improves patient care but also maximizes resource utilization within healthcare facilities.

AI chatbots and virtual assistants have become increasingly common in patient communication. These tools can handle routine inquiries, send appointment reminders, and even assist with basic triage. By automating these processes, healthcare providers can reduce no-show rates, improve patient engagement, and allow staff to focus on more complex patient needs5.

Furthermore, AI systems can adapt in real-time to changes in schedules, such as cancellations or emergencies, automatically rearranging appointments to minimize disruptions and optimize patient flow8.

Clinical Coding and Billing Optimization

Clinical coding and billing are critical processes in healthcare administration, directly impacting reimbursement and financial stability. AI is playing an increasingly important role in optimizing these processes, improving accuracy and efficiency.

AI-powered coding systems can analyze clinical documentation and automatically assign appropriate medical codes. These systems use NLP and machine learning to understand the context of medical records and apply the correct codes based on the latest coding standards. This automation not only speeds up the coding process but also reduces errors that can lead to claim denials or compliance issues6.

In billing optimization, AI algorithms can predict the likelihood of claim denials based on historical data and current coding practices. This predictive capability allows healthcare providers to proactively address potential issues before submitting claims, thereby reducing the rate of denials and improving cash flow9.

Moreover, AI systems can continuously learn from new data, adapting to changes in coding standards and payer requirements. This ensures that the coding and billing processes remain up-to-date and compliant with the latest regulations.

In conclusion, AI is revolutionizing healthcare administration by streamlining documentation, optimizing appointment scheduling, and enhancing coding and billing processes. These advancements not only improve operational efficiency but also contribute to better patient care by allowing healthcare providers to focus more on clinical tasks. As AI technology continues to evolve, we can expect even more innovative solutions to emerge, further transforming the landscape of healthcare administration.

Chapter 9: Resource Management and Optimization

T he healthcare industry is increasingly turning to advanced technologies and data-driven approaches to optimize resource management. This chapter explores three key areas where these innovations are making a significant impact: predictive staffing and resource allocation, supply chain management and inventory optimization, and facility management and predictive maintenance.

Predictive Staffing and Resource Allocation

Predictive staffing is an innovative approach that uses historical data, statistical algorithms, and machine learning techniques to forecast future staffing needs in healthcare settings. This method aims to ensure that the right number of healthcare professionals with the appropriate skills are available at the right time to provide optimal patient care1.

By analyzing various factors such as historical staffing levels, patient admission rates, seasonal trends, and even local events, predictive staffing models can anticipate periods of high or low demand2. For example, these systems might predict an increase in patient numbers due to an upcoming flu season or a local marathon, allowing hospitals to schedule additional staff in advance.

The benefits of predictive staffing are multifaceted. It helps prevent staff burnout by avoiding sudden increases in workload, ensures adequate patient care during peak times, and optimizes resource allocation by preventing overstaffing during quieter periods5. Moreover, by accurately forecasting staffing needs, healthcare organizations can minimize overtime costs and reduce reliance on expensive temporary staff5.

Implementing predictive staffing requires sophisticated software that can integrate data from various sources, including electronic health records, time and attendance systems, and even external data like weather forecasts or local event calendars. While the initial setup may be complex, the long-term benefits in terms of improved patient care, staff satisfaction, and cost savings can be substantial9.

Supply Chain Management and Inventory Optimization

Effective supply chain management is crucial in healthcare to ensure that necessary medical supplies and equipment are available when needed, while also minimizing waste and controlling costs. Inventory optimization is a key component of this process, involving strategies to maintain appropriate stock levels of medical supplies3.

Modern healthcare inventory management systems use data-driven approaches to track and analyze supply usage patterns. These systems can predict future demand, automate reordering processes, and even suggest optimal storage locations for different items3. By leveraging these technologies, healthcare facilities can reduce the risk of supply shortages, prevent the use of expired items, and support evidence-based decisions on medical product selection13.

One innovative approach in healthcare supply chain management is the adoption of lean inventory techniques. This strategy focuses on keeping only the minimum amount of inventory needed to meet demand, thereby reducing carrying costs and minimizing waste7. Advanced analytics and healthcare supply chain software enable accurate demand forecasting, allowing facilities to implement just-in-time inventory practices without compromising patient care7.

Centralized inventory management systems are particularly beneficial for healthcare organizations with multiple departments or facilities. These systems provide real-time visibility of stock levels across the entire organization, enabling more efficient resource allocation and reducing the likelihood of overstocking in one area while another experiences shortages10.

Facility Management and Predictive Maintenance

Facility management in healthcare settings is critical for ensuring a safe, comfortable, and efficient environment for both patients and staff. Predictive maintenance is an advanced approach that uses data-driven techniques to monitor the health of equipment and systems, allowing hospital facilities to address potential issues before they become critical4.

Predictive maintenance relies on sensors, artificial intelligence, and data analytics to monitor equipment in real-time. By analyzing data patterns, these systems can predict when a piece of equipment is likely to fail, allowing maintenance to be scheduled proactively4. This approach is particularly valuable in hospitals, where equipment failures can have immediate and severe consequences for patient care.

The benefits of predictive maintenance in healthcare facilities are numerous. It minimizes equipment downtime, extends the lifespan of critical systems, and allows for better resource allocation by enabling facilities managers to plan maintenance activities during off-peak times4. Moreover, by preventing unexpected breakdowns, predictive maintenance can significantly reduce costs associated with emergency repairs and system downtime8.

Implementing predictive maintenance involves integrating various technologies, including Internet of Things (IoT) devices, machine learning algorithms, and computerized maintenance management systems (CMMS)11. While the initial investment may be substantial, the long-term benefits in terms of improved equipment reliability, reduced maintenance costs, and enhanced patient safety make it an increasingly attractive option for healthcare facilities.

In conclusion, the integration of predictive technologies in staffing, supply chain management, and facility maintenance is transforming resource management in healthcare. By leveraging data and advanced analytics, healthcare organizations can optimize their operations, improve patient care, and achieve significant cost savings. As these technologies continue to evolve, they promise to play an increasingly crucial role in shaping the future of healthcare delivery.

Chapter 10: Ethical Implications of AI in Healthcare

T he integration of Artificial Intelligence (AI) in healthcare brings immense potential for improving patient care, but it also raises significant ethical concerns. This chapter explores three critical ethical implications of AI in healthcare: data privacy and security, bias and fairness in AI algorithms, and transparency and explainability of AI decisions.

Data Privacy and Security

As healthcare organizations increasingly adopt AI technologies, the protection of patient data has become a paramount concern. AI systems require vast amounts of data to function effectively, which raises questions about how this sensitive information is collected, stored, and used6. The consequences of data breaches in healthcare can be severe, potentially leading to identity theft, insurance fraud, or disrupted patient care6.

To address these concerns, healthcare institutions are implementing advanced AI-driven security systems that can proactively monitor data access and detect anomalies in real-time6. These systems not only safeguard patient privacy but also ensure compliance with strict data protection regulations. However, the challenge lies in striking a balance between utilizing data for AI advancement and protecting patient confidentiality.

Lawmakers have emphasized the need for strong federal data privacy protections for consumers as a key component of AI regulation10. As Rep. Frank Pallone, D-N.J., stated, "AI cannot function without large quantities of data. And we must ensure that this increased data demand does not come at the expense of consumers' right to privacy"10. This highlights the ongoing debate about how to regulate AI in healthcare while preserving patient privacy rights.

Bias and Fairness in AI Algorithms

The issue of bias in AI algorithms is a growing concern within healthcare. Bias in this context refers to a difference in performance between subgroups for a predictive task7. For example, an AI algorithm used for predicting future risk of breast cancer may incorrectly assign black patients as "low risk" more often than white patients7.

These biases can stem from various sources, including historical inequities in healthcare access and expenditures, which create spurious associations linking protected class identity to disease outcomes3. The consequences of such biases can be severe, potentially exacerbating existing health disparities and undermining the delivery of equitable care.

To mitigate these biases, strategies such as pre-processing data through sampling, implementing mathematical approaches to incentivize balanced predictions, and post-processing have been proposed7. Additionally, keeping human experts "in the loop" can be crucial in identifying and addressing biases specific to datasets7.

Transparency and Explainability of AI Decisions

The concept of "transparent AI" has emerged as a critical factor in building trust and ensuring accountability in healthcare AI systems. Transparent AI provides insights into its decision-making logic, which is vital for collaboration between human experts and AI tools8.

In a field where mistakes can have significant consequences, transparent AI allows healthcare providers to quickly identify errors and incorrect recommendations, thereby ensuring accountability and preventing potential patient harm8. Moreover, as the healthcare industry is heavily regulated, transparent AI aligns well with regulatory requirements, easing the compliance process for healthcare facilities8.

However, achieving transparency in AI systems can be challenging, particularly with complex deep learning models. The concept of "explainable AI" (XAI) has gained traction as a means to address this issue. XAI aims to make AI decision-making processes understandable to humans, which is crucial for building trust between patients and healthcare providers4.

In conclusion, addressing these ethical implications is crucial for the responsible development and deployment of AI in healthcare. As AI continues to evolve and integrate into healthcare systems, ongoing discussions and collaborations between technologists, healthcare providers, ethicists, and policymakers will be essential to navigate these complex ethical landscapes and ensure that AI truly benefits all patients equitably and ethically.

Chapter 11: Implementation Challenges and Best Practices

―――

The integration of Artificial Intelligence (AI) into healthcare presents significant opportunities for improving patient care and operational efficiency. However, it also comes with notable challenges that need to be addressed for successful implementation. This chapter explores the key challenges and best practices in three critical areas: integrating AI into clinical workflows, training and educating healthcare professionals, and navigating regulatory considerations and compliance.

Integration of AI into Clinical Workflows

Integrating AI into existing clinical workflows is a complex process that requires careful planning and execution. One of the primary challenges is ensuring that AI tools work seamlessly with existing systems, such as Electronic Health Records (EHRs) and practice management software2. This integration involves evaluating compatibility, ensuring smooth data transfer, and maintaining continuity of operations.

A key consideration in this process is data quality and accessibility. Healthcare data is often fragmented across different systems, leading to inaccuracies and inconsistencies that can adversely affect the performance of AI models1. Addressing these data challenges is crucial for the effective implementation of AI in clinical workflows.

Best practices for integration include:

Conducting thorough assessments of existing workflows to identify areas where AI can add value.

Implementing AI solutions gradually, starting with pilot programs in specific departments or for specific tasks.

Ensuring robust data management practices to maintain high-quality, accessible data for AI systems.

Training and Education for Healthcare Professionals

The successful implementation of AI in healthcare heavily depends on the readiness and acceptance of healthcare professionals. However, there is currently a significant skills gap in the workforce regarding the understanding and management of AI technologies[1].

To address this challenge, comprehensive training programs are essential. These programs should focus on:

Developing AI literacy among healthcare professionals, including understanding AI capabilities and limitations.

Providing hands-on experience with AI tools relevant to clinical practice.

Addressing ethical considerations and potential biases in AI systems.

Educational institutions are responding to this need by offering specialized courses in AI for healthcare. For instance, Stanford University and MIT provide robust certifications that cover topics such as predictive analytics, personalized medicine, and clinical data analysis[3].

Regulatory Considerations and Compliance

The regulatory landscape for AI in healthcare is rapidly evolving. Healthcare organizations must stay informed about current and upcoming regulations to ensure compliance and responsible AI implementation.

Key regulatory considerations include:

Data privacy and security: Ensuring compliance with regulations like HIPAA when using AI systems that process patient data[4].

Transparency and explainability: Developing AI systems that can provide insights into their decision-making processes, which is crucial for building trust and ensuring accountability[1].

Fairness and bias mitigation: Implementing strategies to detect and mitigate biases in AI algorithms to ensure equitable healthcare delivery5.

Best practices for regulatory compliance include:

Staying informed about evolving AI regulations in healthcare, such as those outlined in recent executive orders and CMS rules4.

Implementing robust governance frameworks for AI development and deployment.

Regularly auditing AI systems for compliance and performance.

In conclusion, while the integration of AI into healthcare presents significant challenges, these can be overcome through careful planning, comprehensive training, and adherence to regulatory guidelines. By following best practices in these areas, healthcare organizations can harness the full potential of AI to improve patient care and operational efficiency.

Part VI: The Future of AI in Healthcare

Chapter 12: Emerging Trends and Technologies

———

Advances in AI-assisted surgery and robotics

AI in personalized and regenerative medicine

Integration of AI with IoT and 5G technologies. Compose chapters in academic style with Harvard referencing style. Do not use bullet points. Explain terms, concepts and technology so that the non-technical clinical doctor and nurses can understand.

Sources

Answer

Chapter 12: Emerging Trends and Technologies

The future of healthcare is being shaped by rapid advancements in artificial intelligence (AI) and its integration with other cutting-edge technologies. This chapter explores three key areas where AI is poised to make significant impacts: AI-assisted surgery and robotics, personalized and regenerative medicine, and the integration of AI with Internet of Things (IoT) and 5G technologies.

Advances in AI-assisted Surgery and Robotics

AI-assisted surgery and robotics are revolutionizing surgical procedures, offering enhanced precision, reduced invasiveness, and improved patient outcomes. Robotic surgical systems, augmented by AI, are becoming increasingly sophisticated, allowing surgeons to perform complex procedures with greater accuracy and control.

One of the most promising developments in this field is the integration of AI with robotic systems to assist in identifying critical structures, optimizing incision locations, and adapting to patient-specific anatomies during surgery2. This integration enhances the surgeon's capabilities, potentially reducing complications and improving surgical outcomes.

AI is also making significant contributions to preoperative planning and intraoperative guidance. For instance, AI algorithms can analyze patient data and medical imaging to create detailed surgical plans, helping surgeons anticipate potential complications and optimize their approach. During surgery, AI can provide real-time guidance, assisting surgeons in making more informed decisions6.

As these technologies continue to evolve, we can expect to see more autonomous features in surgical robots. While full autonomy is not the goal, robots may be able to perform routine tasks independently, allowing surgeons to focus on more complex aspects of the procedure6. This development could lead to more efficient surgeries and potentially expand access to specialized surgical care.

AI in Personalized and Regenerative Medicine

The intersection of AI and regenerative medicine is creating new possibilities for personalized healthcare. AI's ability to analyze vast amounts of complex data is particularly valuable in this field, where understanding intricate biological processes is crucial.

In stem cell research, AI is playing a critical role in realizing the potential of personalized medicine. By analyzing patient-specific data, AI enables the customization of stem cell therapies to match the unique genetic and molecular profile of each patient7. This bespoke approach not only enhances the effectiveness of treatments but also minimizes the risk of adverse reactions.

AI algorithms are also being used to identify genetic variations linked to specific diseases or treatment responses, enabling the development of personalized treatment plans3. This capability is particularly important in complex, multifactorial diseases where traditional one-size-fits-all approaches are often inadequate.

Furthermore, AI is accelerating drug discovery and development in regenerative medicine. By analyzing vast datasets of genetic and molecular information, AI can identify potential therapeutic targets and predict the efficacy of new treatments, potentially reducing the time and cost of bringing new regenerative therapies to market10.

Integration of AI with IoT and 5G Technologies

The integration of AI with Internet of Things (IoT) devices and 5G networks is set to transform healthcare delivery, enabling more comprehensive and continuous patient care.

5G technology, with its high-speed, low-latency connectivity, is facilitating the integration of IoT devices for remote patient monitoring. Connected sensors, wearables, and medical devices can now transmit real-time health data over 5G networks, enabling continuous monitoring of vital signs, medication adherence, and disease progression4. This capability is particularly valuable for managing chronic conditions and enabling aging in place.

AI plays a crucial role in analyzing the vast amounts of data generated by these connected devices. In 2025, we can expect increased integration of AI with Electronic Health Records (EHRs) to analyze real-time data from wearable devices, allowing for remote monitoring of patients with chronic conditions, detecting anomalies, and providing actionable health insights5.

The combination of AI, IoT, and 5G is also enabling more sophisticated telehealth solutions. Advanced algorithms empowered by these technologies will allow clinicians to assess patients virtually with greater accuracy, potentially expanding access to specialized care for underserved or rural communities5.

In conclusion, the future of AI in healthcare promises significant advancements in surgical precision, personalized medicine, and connected health solutions. As these technologies continue to evolve and integrate, they have the potential to dramatically improve patient outcomes, enhance the efficiency of healthcare delivery, and expand access to high-quality care. However, it's important to note that while AI and related technologies offer powerful tools, they are designed to augment, not replace, the expertise of healthcare professionals. The human touch in healthcare remains irreplaceable, with AI serving as a valuable aid in decision-making and patient care.

Chapter 13: Preparing for an AI-Enabled Healthcare Future

As artificial intelligence (AI) continues to transform healthcare, it is crucial for healthcare professionals to adapt and prepare for an AI-enabled future. This chapter explores three key aspects of this preparation: developing AI literacy among healthcare professionals, fostering collaborative approaches to AI development and implementation, and balancing innovation with patient safety and care quality.

Developing AI Literacy in Healthcare Professionals

AI literacy in healthcare refers to the ability of medical professionals to understand, interpret, and effectively use AI technologies in clinical practice. It is not about becoming AI developers, but rather about gaining the knowledge and skills necessary to integrate AI tools into patient care responsibly and effectively7.

To address the growing need for AI literacy, educational institutions and professional organizations are developing comprehensive AI training programs for healthcare professionals. These programs focus on understanding AI technologies, interpreting AI-generated results, and integrating AI into clinical workflows1. For instance, the Medical AI Literacy Course offers a comprehensive e-learning program designed to equip healthcare professionals with the knowledge and skills necessary to harness the full potential of AI in their practice3.

However, implementing AI education in healthcare faces several challenges, including time constraints, overburdened curricula, and a shortage of qualified educators1. To overcome these barriers, collaborative efforts among AI developers, professional societies, and academic institutions are necessary to design comprehensive and accessible AI training programs.

Collaborative Approaches to AI Development and Implementation

The successful integration of AI into healthcare requires a collaborative approach that involves diverse stakeholders, including healthcare professionals, patients, AI developers, and policymakers. This collaborative model ensures that AI solutions are developed and implemented in ways that address real healthcare needs and align with ethical and clinical standards.

One promising approach is the community-driven co-development of ethical AI healthcare solutions. This method emphasizes bottom-up decision-making to reflect and center the needs and values of impacted communities2. By involving patients, healthcare providers, and other stakeholders in the AI development process, we can create more equitable and effective AI solutions that serve patient and community needs.

Collaborative models such as federated learning and open datasets are also emerging as ways to foster innovation while addressing privacy concerns4. These approaches allow for the sharing of insights and data across institutions without compromising patient privacy, paving the way for a more collaborative and innovative healthcare ecosystem.

Balancing Innovation with Patient Safety and Care Quality

While AI offers tremendous potential for improving healthcare, it is crucial to balance innovation with patient safety and care quality. This balance requires careful consideration of ethical implications, regulatory compliance, and the integration of AI into existing clinical workflows.

One key aspect of maintaining this balance is ensuring transparency and explainability in AI systems. Healthcare providers need to understand how AI algorithms arrive at their conclusions to build trust and ensure accountability1. This transparency is crucial for identifying potential biases or errors in AI-generated recommendations and maintaining the quality of patient care.

Another important consideration is the implementation of human-in-the-loop approaches, where AI systems support, rather than replace, clinical decision-making2. This approach ensures that human judgment and expertise remain central to patient care, with AI serving as a powerful tool to augment and enhance clinical decision-making.

Regulatory frameworks also play a crucial role in balancing innovation with patient safety. These frameworks must be anticipatory and represent diverse stakeholders to ensure that AI development in healthcare is driven by patient needs rather than profit alone2.

In conclusion, preparing for an AI-enabled healthcare future requires a multifaceted approach that includes developing AI literacy among healthcare professionals, fostering collaborative approaches to AI development and implementation, and carefully balancing innovation with patient safety and care quality. By addressing these key areas, we can harness the full potential of AI to improve patient outcomes and transform healthcare delivery while maintaining the highest standards of care and ethical practice.

Frequently Asked Questions (FAQ) on AI in Healthcare

W hat is artificial intelligence in healthcare?

Artificial intelligence in healthcare refers to the use of machine learning algorithms and other AI technologies to analyze complex medical data, assist in clinical decision-making, and improve patient care outcomes1.

How is AI being used in medical imaging?

AI is being used in radiology, pathology, and dermatology to analyze medical images, detect abnormalities, and assist in diagnosis. For example, AI algorithms can analyze X-rays, CT scans, and MRIs to identify potential diseases or conditions4.

What are some challenges in implementing AI in healthcare?

Key challenges include data quality and security, integration with existing systems, regulatory compliance, building trust among patients and healthcare providers, and addressing potential biases in AI algorithms46.

How can healthcare professionals prepare for an AI-enabled future?

Healthcare professionals can prepare by developing AI literacy through specialized training programs, participating in collaborative AI development efforts, and staying informed about emerging AI technologies and their applications in healthcare1.

What are the ethical considerations in using AI for healthcare?

Ethical considerations include ensuring patient privacy and data security, addressing potential biases in AI algorithms, maintaining transparency in AI decision-making processes, and balancing innovation with patient safety and care quality4.

How is AI improving clinical decision support?

AI-powered clinical decision support tools can analyze patient data, medical literature, and clinical guidelines to provide real-time recommendations to healthcare providers, potentially improving diagnostic accuracy and treatment planning1.

What role does AI play in personalized medicine?

AI helps analyze large-scale genomic and molecular data to identify personalized treatment options, predict disease risks, and optimize drug therapies for individual patients1.

How is AI transforming healthcare administration?

AI is streamlining administrative processes through automated documentation, optimized appointment scheduling, and improved clinical coding and billing practices4.

What is the future of AI in surgery and robotics?

AI is enhancing surgical precision through robotic systems, improving preoperative planning, and providing real-time guidance during procedures. Future developments may include more autonomous features in surgical robots1.

How does AI contribute to remote patient care?

AI enables advanced telemedicine solutions, powers virtual health assistants, and analyzes data from wearable devices for continuous patient monitoring and early detection of health issues2.

What are the regulatory considerations for AI in healthcare?

Healthcare organizations must ensure compliance with data privacy laws like HIPAA, adhere to ethical guidelines, and stay informed about evolving AI regulations in healthcare4.

How can healthcare organizations address AI implementation costs?

Organizations can explore partnerships, utilize cloud computing and managed services, and focus on long-term cost savings and operational efficiencies to offset initial investments in AI implementation4.

What is the role of AI in drug discovery and development?

AI accelerates drug discovery by analyzing vast datasets of genetic and molecular information to identify potential therapeutic targets and predict the efficacy of new treatments1.

How can healthcare providers build trust in AI systems?

Providers can build trust by ensuring transparency in AI decision-making processes, involving stakeholders in AI development and implementation, and educating both patients and healthcare professionals about AI capabilities and limitations4.

What is the importance of interdisciplinary collaboration in healthcare AI?

Interdisciplinary collaboration brings together expertise from medicine, data science, engineering, and healthcare administration, fostering innovation and ensuring that AI solutions address real-world healthcare needs effectively4.

Glossary of Terms

Artificial Intelligence (AI): The simulation of human intelligence processes by machines, especially computer systems.

Machine Learning (ML): A subset of AI that enables systems to learn and improve from experience without being explicitly programmed.

Deep Learning: A type of machine learning based on artificial neural networks with multiple layers.

Natural Language Processing (NLP): A branch of AI that deals with the interaction between computers and humans using natural language.

Computer Vision: A field of AI that trains computers to interpret and understand the visual world.

Predictive Analytics: The use of data, statistical algorithms, and machine learning techniques to identify the likelihood of future outcomes based on historical data.

Electronic Health Records (EHR): Digital versions of patients' paper charts that make information available instantly and securely to authorized users.

Telemedicine: The practice of caring for patients remotely when the provider and patient are not physically present with each other.

Wearable Devices: Electronic devices that can be worn as accessories, embedded in clothing, implanted in the user's body, or even tattooed on the skin.

Internet of Things (IoT): The interconnection via the internet of computing devices embedded in everyday objects, enabling them to send and receive data.

5G: The fifth generation technology standard for broadband cellular networks, providing faster speeds and more reliable connections.

Precision Medicine: An approach to patient care that allows doctors to select treatments based on a genetic understanding of their disease.

Genomics: The study of all of a person's genes (the genome), including interactions of those genes with each other and with the person's environment.

Proteomics: The large-scale study of proteins, particularly their structures and functions.

Clinical Decision Support Systems (CDSS): Computer systems designed to assist healthcare professionals in making clinical decisions.

Federated Learning: A machine learning technique that trains an algorithm across multiple decentralized devices or servers holding local data samples, without exchanging them.

Explainable AI (XAI): Artificial intelligence systems whose actions can be easily understood by humans.

Bias in AI: Systematic errors in AI systems that can lead to unfair outcomes for certain groups of people.

HIPAA: The Health Insurance Portability and Accountability Act, a US law designed to provide privacy standards to protect patients' medical records and other health information.

Robotics in Healthcare: The use of robots in various healthcare settings, from surgical assistance to patient care and rehabilitation.

Regenerative Medicine: A branch of medicine that develops methods to regrow, repair or replace damaged or diseased cells, organs or tissues.

Personalized Medicine: A medical model that separates people into different groups—with medical decisions, practices, interventions and/or products being tailored to the individual patient based on their predicted response or risk of disease.

Chatbot: A computer program designed to simulate conversation with human users, especially over the Internet.

Blockchain in Healthcare: The use of blockchain technology to securely store and manage health data.

Virtual Reality (VR) in Healthcare: The use of computer technology to create a simulated environment for medical training, therapy, or patient education.

Augmented Reality (AR) in Healthcare: Technology that superimposes a computer-generated image on a user's view of the real world, used in medical education and surgical planning.

Big Data in Healthcare: Extremely large data sets that may be analyzed computationally to reveal patterns, trends, and associations, especially relating to human behavior and interactions in health contexts.

Cloud Computing in Healthcare: The delivery of different services through the Internet, including data storage, servers, databases, networking, and software.

Interoperability: The ability of different information systems, devices or applications to connect, exchange data, and use the information that has been exchanged.

Population Health Management: The aggregation of patient data across multiple health information technology resources, the analysis of that data into a single, actionable patient record, and the actions through which care providers can improve both clinical and financial outcomes.

Digital Therapeutics: Evidence-based therapeutic interventions driven by high-quality software programs to prevent, manage, or treat a medical disorder or disease.

Health Information Exchange (HIE): The mobilization of healthcare information electronically across organizations within a region, community or hospital system.

Cybersecurity in Healthcare: The practice of protecting systems, networks, and programs from digital attacks in healthcare settings.

Remote Patient Monitoring (RPM): The use of digital technologies to collect medical and other forms of health data from individuals in one location and electronically transmit that information securely to healthcare providers in a different location for assessment and recommendations.

Quantum Computing in Healthcare: The use of quantum-mechanical phenomena such as superposition and entanglement to perform computation, potentially revolutionizing drug discovery and personalized medicine.